T0273601

Astrology

Secrets of the Signs and Planets

Publisher & Creative Director: Nick Wells
Editorial Director: Catherine Taylor
Art Director: Mike Spender
Digital Design & Production: Chris Herbert

Special thanks to: Anna Groves, Dawn Laker, Frances Bodiam
and the artists who allowed us to reproduce their work.

FLAME TREE PUBLISHING

6 Melbray Mews, Fulham,
London SW6 3NS, United Kingdom
www.flametreepublishing.com

First published 2022
22 24 26 25 23
1 3 5 7 9 10 8 6 4 2
ISBN: 978-1-80417-235-3

Printed in China | Created, Developed & Produced in the United Kingdom

Astrology

Secrets of the Signs and Planets

Victor Olliver

Foreword by Shelley von Strunckel

FLAME TREE
PUBLISHING

Contents

Foreword 6

Introduction 8

Star Signs and the Zodiac 12

Signs: Energies and Qualities. 26

The Horoscope Chart: What Is It?. 36

Chart Houses 44

The Planets. 54

Personality and Career 64

The Aspects 72

How to Read a Horoscope 80

Charts of Famous People 94

Forecasting. 102

Retrogrades 114

Astrology Online. .120

Further Resources. 124

Acknowledgments .126

Foreword

ASTROLOGY. That single word sparks passionate exchanges, between its fans and devotees, who derive comfort and guidance from it, and those who loudly decry it as 'mumbo jumbo' (but who, oddly, can't resist reading what their stars hold for them).

Few are aware that astrology evolved when knowledge of the heavens was part of everyday life: this knowledge directed nomadic tribes and led them to rivers and wells. As humanity settled and learned to grow their food, studying the link between the Sun's yearly cycle and the seasons was again vital to life. But early humans found even more to fascinate them in the skies, and their observations of the Sun, the Moon and, of course, the stars led to the cultivation of deities – the constellations that became the zodiac signs.

Today's astrology still focuses on those heavenly star signs and, for such an archaic tradition, is immensely popular. There are endless columns, offering

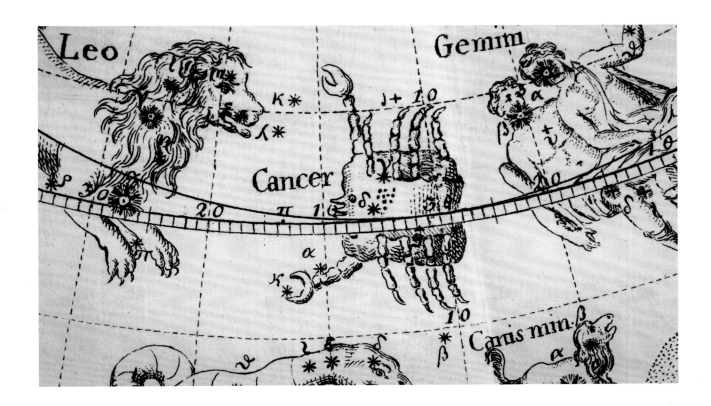

predictions for the day, the week, the month and the year. Perhaps nowadays there is more emphasis on which signs are destined for love, happiness or personal gain, but whether people are seeking romantic, financial or professional guidance, there is a vast array of columns offering all manner of life advice.

In this book, Victor Olliver touches on astrology's historical journey, from its early days to the latest online astro-predictions. He then gives detailed and clear explanations of the workings of astrology, including how a personal astrological chart (or horoscope) is made, how it can reveal an individual's character and, when linked to the current or future planetary set-up, their future.

Seeking an overview? This is your book. Want in-depth knowledge? This is your jumping-off point. Want to justify your interest in astrology to doubters? It's all here, clearly explained.

What's more, in addition to being a true astrological expert, Victor writes with a Gemini's deeply diving curiosity for the subject. And finally, this book is gorgeous to look at.

Shelley von Strunckel

Introduction

Astrology has never been more popular than it is today. One poll says that over 90 per cent of people know their star sign – test this by asking your friends. In the US alone, nearly 30 per cent of people say they 'believe' in astrology. And really, who can resist reading their stars?

For over 5000 years people have consulted the planets and stars for guidance on their love lives, health, finances and careers – but most of all for forecasts of the future. No one can explain why astrology works, but ancient civilizations were the first to notice a connection between human events and the position of celestial objects in the heavens.

Powerful People Have Long Used Astrology

Astrology originated in ancient Mesopotamia and migrated to Egypt before being taken up by Persia, Greece, Rome and India. The Roman emperor Tiberius (42 BCE–37 CE) had a court astrologer called Thrasyllus. This man correctly forecast that Tiberius, even when his succession looked unlikely, would be the next emperor.

'Astrology is just a finger pointing at reality.'

Steven Forrest, American astrologer, author and lecturer

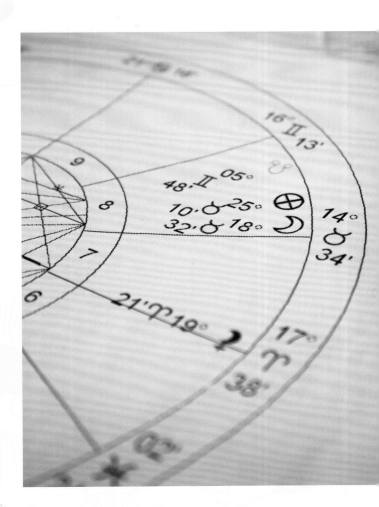

In England's Tudor period, Queen Elizabeth I (1533–1603) consulted her personal astrologer John Dee to select the right moment for her coronation in 1559.

In modern times, the astrologer Joan Quigley controlled the schedules of US President Ronald Reagan and First Lady Nancy Reagan. 'I read the President's horoscope hourly, for political reasons as well as for safety,' Quigley wrote in her memoir, *What Does Joan Say?* (*See* page 112.)

Celebrities Look to the Stars

Today, a great many celebrities use astrology. In 2019 US 'Princess of Pop' Britney Spears (a Sagittarius) posted on Instagram that she was seeking healing insights from Jan Spiller's bestselling book *Astrology for the Soul.*

In that year, singer-songwriter Taylor Swift (also Sagittarius) told *Rolling Stone* magazine that she and fellow star Katy Perry (Scorpio) had healed a rift by talking about how their star signs can misunderstand each other.

What Astrology Aims to Do

Astrology analyses human character and makes predictions. It is a symbolic language built up from ancient ideas and religious beliefs. By the end of this book, you will have enough basic information to cast your own horoscope on free online websites, and to read the charts of loved ones, friends (and enemies!).

'I'm living proof of all life's contradictions…I'm a Pisces fish and the river runs through my soul.'

George Harrison,
song 'Pisces Fish'

Star Signs and the Zodiac

Astrology reveals amazing information about people and events through the observation of the movements and positions of planets in our solar system. Even asteroids and distant stars, once placed in a horoscope chart, can communicate fascinating details.

Astrology starts with what is probably best known and understood about astrology – the 12 star (or, more properly, 'Sun') signs, Aries to Pisces.

These 12 signs fill the zodiac, which is a narrow band that marks the pathway of the Sun (known as the 'ecliptic') as it appears to orbit the Earth. Of course, we know the opposite is true and that the Earth orbits the Sun, but in astrology our interest is in how things appear to be, not necessarily as they are scientifically.

'We need not feel ashamed of flirting with the zodiac. The zodiac is well worth flirting with.'

D.H. Lawrence, English writer

What Are the Zodiac Signs?

The signs are based on star constellations many light-years away that fall within this zodiac band. Over one year, the Sun moves through all the signs, spending about four weeks in each.

Your star sign is determined by where the Sun was in the zodiac at the time of your birth. Each sign occupies 30 degrees of the sky. Multiply that by the 12 signs and you get 360 degrees – a complete circle (the zodiac). It is this that is the basis of the horoscope chart wheel.

The 12 Zodiac Star (or Sun) Signs

Each zodiac sign represents certain human characteristics, and each has traditional associations, with body parts and even with plants and flowers. Below are the 12 signs with dates, symbols and a brief description of their characteristics, along with the planet that 'rules' (or is associated with) each sign.

ARIES
21 March–20 April

The Ram: The first zodiac sign.

Characteristics: Bold, bossy and decisive. Highly competitive and easily bored. Likes to be Number One and the leader of the pack. Will not take 'No' for an answer. An Aries gets things done. Ruled by Mars and is associated with the head.

Lucky flower/plant: Honeysuckle.

Famous Aries people: Elton John, Diana Ross, Leonardo da Vinci, Charlie Chaplin, Lady Gaga, Aretha Franklin.

'Anyone can be a millionaire, but to become a billionaire you need an astrologer.'

J.P. Morgan, American financier and an Aries

TAURUS
21 April–21 May

The Bull: The second zodiac sign.

Characteristics: Extravagant, sensual, stubborn. Desires stability. Has an awesome anger (though is slow to rouse) and is a hard worker. Dedicated, dependable and is quietly determined. Ruled by Venus and is associated with the neck, throat and shoulders.

Lucky flower/plant: Rose.

Famous Taurus people: William Shakespeare, Queen Elizabeth II, Barbra Streisand, Adolf Hitler, Audrey Hepburn, Shirley Temple.

'Astrology is one of the most ancient sciences, held in high esteem of old, by the wise and great. Formerly no prince would make war or peace, nor any general fight a battle, in short no important affair was undertaken without first consulting an astrologer.'

Benjamin Franklin (1751)

GEMINI

22 May–21 June

The Twins: The third zodiac sign.

Characteristics: Chatty, curious, fickle. Usually clever or quick and gossipy. Easily bored, a Gemini needs constant mental stimulation and a fast-paced life. Not the best keeper of secrets. Ruled by Mercury and is associated with the arms and nerves.

Lucky flower/plant: Lavender.

Famous Gemini people: Bob Dylan, Queen Victoria, John F. Kennedy, Paul McCartney, Prince, Marilyn Monroe.

CANCER

22 June–23 July

The Crab: The fourth zodiac sign.

Characteristics: Nurturing, moody, highly sensitive. Has a long memory. Kind and considerate and likes to be surrounded by friends and family. High emotional

intelligence. Ruled by Moon and is associated with the chest and breasts.

Lucky flower/plant: White roses.

Famous Cancer people: Diana, Princess of Wales, Meryl Streep, Alexander the Great, Julius Caesar, Henry VIII, Nelson Mandela.

LEO
24 July–23 August

The Lion: The fifth zodiac sign.

Characteristics: Theatrical, proud, protective.

Demands attention, offers and demands loyalty. Excellent managers, ambitious, noisy and very entertaining. Ruled by Sun and is associated with the heart and spine.

Lucky flower/plant: Sunflower.

Famous Leo people: Napoleon Bonaparte, Barack Obama, Whitney Houston, Mata Hari, Henry Ford, Madonna.

VIRGO

24 August–23 September

The Maiden: The sixth zodiac sign.

Characteristics: Analytical, practical, caring and discreet. Fault-finders. Prone to stress-related conditions and taking on other people's problems. Ruled by Mercury and is associated with the abdomen, liver and pancreas.

Lucky flower/plant: Chrysanthemum.

Famous Virgo people: Queen Elizabeth I, Michael Jackson, Stephen King, Lyndon B. Johnson, Sean Connery, Mother Teresa.

LIBRA

24 September–23 October

The Scales: The seventh zodiac sign.

Characteristics: Charming, diplomatic, ready to compromise. Will try to keep the peace. Drawn to the arts and beauty in general. A natural negotiator. Ruled by Venus and is associated with the lower back and kidneys.

Lucky flower/plant: Freesia.

Famous Libra people: Mahatma Gandhi, Oscar Wilde, Margaret Thatcher, Jimmy Carter, Emperor Augustus, Julie Andrews.

SCORPIO

24 October–22 November

The Scorpion: The eighth zodiac sign.

Characteristics: Insightful, secretive, passionate. Excellent at planning and plotting. Seeks authenticity and is unafraid of upsetting people in argument. Co-ruled by Mars and Pluto and is associated with the reproductive organs.

Lucky flower/plant: Venus flytrap.

Famous Scorpio people: Bill Gates, Christopher Columbus, Theodore Roosevelt, Indira Gandhi, Marie Antoinette, Whoopie Goldberg.

SAGITTARIUS

23 November–21 December

The Archer: The ninth zodiac sign.

Characteristics: Adventurous, philosophical, indiscreet. Independent and comic. Can be hugely

indiscreet but only because intolerant of hypocrisy. Party people. Ruled by Jupiter and is associated with thighs and legs.

Lucky flower/plant: Carnation.

Famous Sagittarius people: Steven Spielberg, Winston Churchill, Tina Turner, Frank Sinatra, Walt Disney, Mary, Queen of Scots.

CAPRICORN
22 December–20 January

The Goat: The tenth zodiac sign.

Characteristics: Ambitious, goal-oriented, organized. Has no time for dreamers. Sense of humour tends to be on the dark side. Born to run establishments but prone to pessimism. Ruled by Saturn and is associated with bones, knees and skin.

Lucky flower/plant: Pansy.

Famous Capricorn people: David Bowie, Dolly Parton, Elvis Presley, Marlene Dietrich, Joan of Arc, Martin Luther King Jr.

AQUARIUS
21 January–19 February

The Water-Bearer: The eleventh zodiac sign.

Characteristics: Rebellious, sociable, intellectual. Ardently independent and unpredictable. Can be inflexible. Prone to sudden 'Eureka!' moments. Great fun. Ruled by Uranus and is associated with ankles and blood vessels.

Lucky flower/plant: Orchid.

Famous Aquarius people: Abraham Lincoln, Ronald Reagan, John Travolta, Virginia Woolf, Oprah Winfrey, Bob Marley.

PISCES
20 February–20 March

The Fishes: The twelfth zodiac sign.

Characteristics: Dreamy, intuitive, sympathetic. The listeners of the zodiac. Though seemingly vague at times, can be surprisingly resolute once set on a course of action. Ruled by Neptune and is associated with feet.

Lucky flower/plant: Water lily.

Famous Pisces people: Albert Einstein, Rupert Murdoch, Elizabeth Taylor, Osama bin Laden, Steve Jobs, Liza Minnelli.

National Character

Each nation has a star sign. This is determined by the moment the country is 'born' or becomes independent. Nicholas Campion's *The Book of World Horoscopes* contains every national chart. For example:

Australia and Spain
Sagittarius – outspoken and embracing

Egypt and Morocco
Pisces – influenced by the spiritual

France and China
Libra – seeks to negotiate

Iceland and Argentina
Gemini – endlessly curious

Israel and South Africa
Taurus – strong on financial matters

New Zealand and India
Aquarius – keen on innovations

USA and Italy
Cancer – develops powerful loyalties

UK and Germany
Capricorn – has a love of tradition

Signs: Energies and Qualities

The Sun signs are a starting point for understanding ourselves. What is less known is that each zodiac sign is based on natural energies and qualities, all of which tell us yet more about the kind of people we are.

Our Elemental Nature

Firstly, each zodiac Sun sign is an expression of one of the four elements – fire, earth, air and water. The signs are grouped three per element, making four groupings called 'triplicities'. Elementally, the signs are grouped in the following way, each with positive and negative characteristics.

Fire

This is the element that influences Aries, Leo and Sagittarius.

☀ **Positive:** Creative, bold, passionate. Carried by strong ideas, faith or intuition.

☀ **Negative:** Brash, egotistical, indiscreet.

Earth

This is the element that influences Taurus, Virgo and Capricorn.

☀ **Positive:** Practical, steadfast, sensual. Driven by material or career ambitions.

☀ **Negative:** Greedy, selfish, stubborn.

'We are born at a given moment, in a given place and, like vintage years of wine, we have the qualities of the year and of the season of which we are born. Astrology does not lay claim to anything more.'

Carl Gustav Jung,
Swiss psychiatrist and psychoanalyst

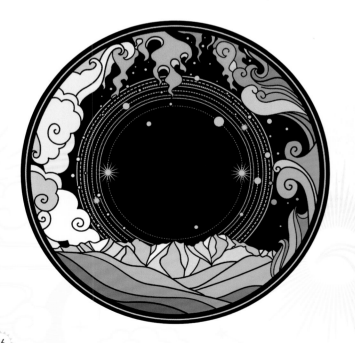

Air

This is the element that influences Gemini, Libra and Aquarius.

- ☀ **Positive**: Intellectual, communicative, objective. Galvanized by big ideas.
- ☀ **Negative**: Heartless, over-idealistic, dogmatic.

Water

This is the element that influences Cancer, Scorpio and Pisces.

- ☀ **Positive**: Empathetic, shrewd, imaginative. Inspired by soulful influences.
- ☀ **Negative**: Sentimental, self-pitying, hyper-sensitive.

A Mixed Bag of Energies

Bear in mind that these descriptions do not fully describe all people in each sign. All of us are a mixture of positive and negative traits. When we get to the horoscope sections of this book, we shall see that other factors also help to decide whether we are, for example, 'earthy' or 'airy' types.

Our Human Qualities

Secondly, the 12 Sun signs are grouped according to their human qualities – cardinal, fixed and mutable. These qualities are called 'modalities' and help us to understand in more detail the kind of person you

are. These three groupings are called 'quadruplicities' because there are four signs per quality. Here are the three groups with a short description of their signs.

Cardinal

The modality of Aries, Cancer, Libra and Capricorn.

Cardinal means the leader or 'the first'. This is because each of these signs marks the start of a season: Aries starts spring, Cancer summer, Libra autumn (or fall) and Capricorn winter. These are the seasonal points in the world's northern hemisphere (e.g., the USA, Europe and the UK).

Cardinal types are people who start things, who have a great deal of personal initiative and lead the way. They are competitive and like to be the best.

Fixed

The modality of Taurus, Leo, Scorpio and Aquarius.

This energy gets things done by being resolute and determined. The fixed signs are associated with stabilizing situations and have a reputation for being reliable and trustworthy. These are mid-season star signs: Taurus in spring, Leo in summer, Scorpio in autumn and Aquarius in winter (again, in the northern hemisphere).

Fixed types are people who often manage other's ideas and initiatives. Without them, nothing would ever get past the ideas stage.

Mutable

The modality of Gemini, Virgo, Sagittarius and Pisces.

Mutable means flexible and adaptable. This energy is highly responsive to change and challenge. There is a lot of spontaneity. Each mutable sign marks the last stage of a season: Gemini in spring, Virgo in summer, Sagittarius in autumn and Pisces in winter (northern hemisphere).

'The modalities of the zodiac symbolize three universal
life conditions: creation (cardinal), preservation (fixed),
and transformation (mutable).'

SirCheo, American astrologer and psychic empath

Mutable types are people who think things through, who educate and communicate. They tend to philosophize and prepare people for turning points in their lives.

We Are Not Just One Quality

As with the elements, each person is not exclusively cardinal, fixed or mutable. We are all a mixture of qualities. But when we examine a person's birth horoscope, we can work out which quality is the major one, according to where all the planets are in the signs – as we shall see later in this book.

Masculine and Feminine Energies

Thirdly, the signs are divided into two groups known as 'dualities' – masculine and feminine. These energies exist in all of us and describe how we experience the world and interact with it. They have nothing to do with one's biological or self-identified gender or sexual orientation. You may be a man with a great deal of feminine energy or a woman with much masculine energy. In most people there is a mixture of the masculine (outward expression) and feminine (inner expression). Here are the two groups and their signs:

Masculine Energy
Aries, Gemini, Leo, Libra, Sagittarius and Aquarius.

These are fire signs (Aries, Leo and Sagittarius) and air signs (Gemini, Libra and Aquarius). The energy is direct, active and impactful. The expression of these signs is outward and engaged with the world.

Feminine Energy
Taurus, Cancer, Virgo, Scorpio, Capricorn and Pisces.

These are earth signs (Taurus, Virgo and Capricorn) and water signs (Cancer, Scorpio and Pisces). The energy is receptive, self-contained and soulful. The expression of these signs is inward and engaged with one's own ideas and dreams.

The Cosmic Pairings of Signs

The zodiac has 'polarities' – or cosmic pairs where two signs sit directly opposite each other in the horoscope, 180 degrees apart. These opposites are not hostile to each other, instead each cosmic pair represents different ways of expressing certain shared or similar energies.

> '**I believe in astrology and the spirits. I am a Virgo myself.**'
>
> Peter Sellers, English actor

Here are the six pairs or polarities, each with its associated life themes.

Aries and Libra
Ego and relationships: Aries self-asserts; Libra compromises.

Taurus and Scorpio
Money and moral values: Taurus is self-directed and principled; Scorpio shares and transforms.

Gemini and Sagittarius
Mind and education: Gemini is curious; Sagittarius commits to an idea.

Cancer and Capricorn

Family versus work: Cancer nurtures; Capricorn earns.

Leo and Aquarius

The personal and impersonal: Leo displays;
Aquarius campaigns.

Virgo and Pisces

Material and spiritual lives: Virgo analyses; Pisces dreams.

Stay Healthy

A deeper understanding of our star signs
can help us better manage our wellbeing
and be more attentive to what our minds
and bodies need to stay healthy.

Aries
Competitive games can help
alleviate stress from torpor.

Taurus
Self-indulgent luxuries to raise the spirits.

Gemini
Lively conversation to
keep the brain buzzing.

Cancer
Family get-togethers to give
a sense of belonging.

The Horoscope Chart: What Is It?

The horoscope is also called the birth or natal chart and is a snapshot of where the planets were in the zodiac at the moment of your birth. This tells the astrologer many things about you.

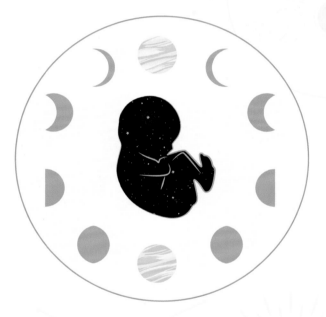

'I was born during an eclipse.
I believe very much in astrology.
If you were born on an eclipse it
indicates your destiny is chaotic.'

Gloria Vanderbilt,
American heiress and socialite

Your birth chart is a unique and symbolic map of you. It reveals the kind of person you are, your personality, likes and dislikes, talents, weaknesses, wealth and health potential, and the kind of people you are drawn to.

Predictions and Free Will

From the horoscope it is also possible to forecast the sort of opportunities and challenges you will face in life – though it is important to remember that everyone has free will. We are not cosmic puppets. We can decide to make the most of life or not, though certain events are sometimes unavoidable.

How the Horoscope Is Created

All this is possible by seeing where the planets are positioned in your horoscope. To create the chart, we start with your time, date and place of birth. It is still possible to read a person's horoscope without the precise time of their birth, but the chart will miss a few important details.

Astrologers used to cast charts by hand using a complex mathematical formula. But these days a horoscope can be created with the aid of astrological software programs, once all the birth data has been entered.

'I don't believe in astrology. I'm a Sagittarius and we are sceptical.'

Arthur C. Clarke, English science-fiction writer

A Guide to What Is Where in a Horoscope

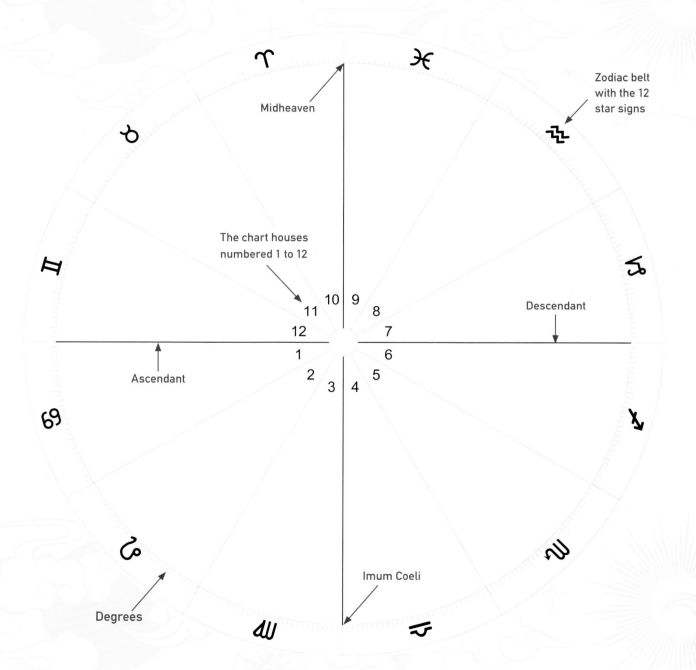

Midheaven

Zodiac belt with the 12 star signs

The chart houses numbered 1 to 12

Descendant

Ascendant

Imum Coeli

Degrees

What the Horoscope Contains

A horoscope resembles a cosmic clock and comprises the following. (See also the chart illustration opposite which shows where these elements are to be found in the wheel.)

The Zodiac

This is the outer wheel belt with the 12 star (or Sun) sign symbols running anti-clockwise.

The Houses

The horoscope is divided into 12 sections called 'houses', each representing different life themes, such as money (the second house) or relationships (the seventh house). Each house corresponds to one of the zodiac signs (such as Aries with the first house or Capricorn with the tenth house). We shall look at chart houses in more detail in the next chapter.

The Degrees

These run on the inside line of the zodiac belt. We saw earlier that the horoscope is a 360-degree wheel. Degrees are used to accurately locate a planet according to its actual position in the sky; this can be calculated by software programs. The degrees also tell us how far apart the planets are from each other, which is significant, as we shall see later. Like each of the zodiac signs, each house occupies a 30-degree section of the horoscope.

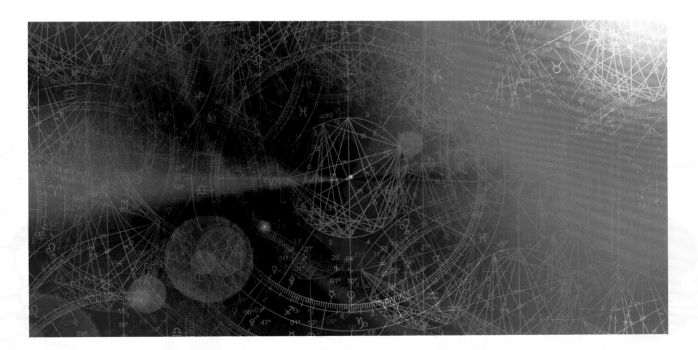

The Horoscope's Four Fateful 'Points'

These four points relate to different life areas, and each is coloured and shaped by the zodiac sign it occupies.

- ☀ **The Ascendant** symbolizes the self or personality.
- ☀ **The Descendant** describes the people we are drawn to.
- ☀ **The Midheaven** represents life direction or career potential.
- ☀ **The Imum Coeli** signifies a person's family, roots and personal life.

The Chart's Four Fateful Hemispheres

The horoscope is divided into four separate areas, each revealing more information about you.

☀ **The Southern Hemisphere**

The top half of the chart represents the public, outside world. A chart with many planets in this sector reveals that the person is highly sociable and very involved in public duties. Quite the extrovert.

☀ **The Northern Hemisphere**

The bottom half of the chart represents our private life. A chart with many planets in this sector reveals that the person is probably preoccupied with personal or family matters and may be a little introverted.

☀ The Eastern Hemisphere

The left-hand half of the chart represents personal power. A chart with many planets in this sector reveals that the person is highly driven and assertive, motivated by their own ideas and may be quite independent.

☀ The Western Hemisphere

The right-hand half of the chart represents the power we give to others. A chart with many planets in this section reveals that the person is very receptive to other people's ideas, will be a people-pleaser and may feel more comfortable working in joint or group ventures.

Most people's charts have planets in different parts of the horoscope and so exhibit a mixture of characteristics.

Stay Healthy

Here are a few more suggested exercises, mental and physical, with the signs that will benefit from them most.

Leo
An appreciative audience to feel loved.

Virgo
Mental challenges to dodge lethargic doldrums.

Libra
Places of beauty to delight the eye and soul.

Scorpio
Any kind of mystery exercises the mind.

Chart Houses

The horoscope covers all aspects of life – from work and finances to love and family – and it does so through the 12 chart houses. Each house covers a wide variety of topics under a main theme.

Interpreting the meaning of each planet depends on which chart house it is in. For instance, Venus in the first house has a different focus from Venus in the eighth house. Before we examine the symbolism of the planets, here is a brief guide to what each house represents.

The First House

Main theme: The self – 'It's all about me.'

Associated with the dynamic energies of Aries and Mars. This house focuses on 'you' – on your physical appearance, personality, basic character traits, vitality, health and the way you talk and act. It also covers the 'firsts' in life, such as new business ventures or anything being initiated by you.

'What it boils down to is that each person has his own ways of coping with trauma and grief, with the pain of life, and astrology was one of mine.'

Nancy Reagan, First Lady of the United States

The Second House

Main theme:

Value and values – 'What am I worth?'

Associated with the life-affirming energies of Taurus and Venus. This house is a lot about the things we appreciate, such as our five senses, money, asset value, material possessions and income. It is also about how we value ourselves, raising matters to do with self-esteem, confidence and returns for work. Moral values are also included.

The Third House

Main theme:

Communication – 'I have something to tell you.'

Associated with the sharing energies of Gemini and Mercury. This house includes the many ways we interact with others and the information that we share in our words, emails and letters. In another sense, this is the house of your local neighbourhood and your neighbours, brothers and sisters, short journeys, newspapers and contracts.

The Fourth House

Main theme:

Home and family – 'Be part of my gang.'

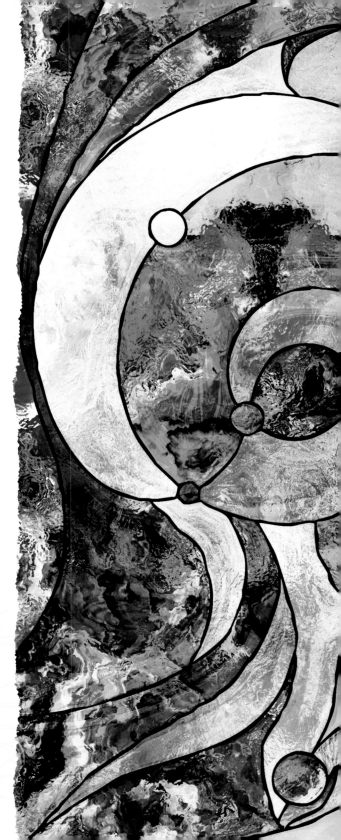

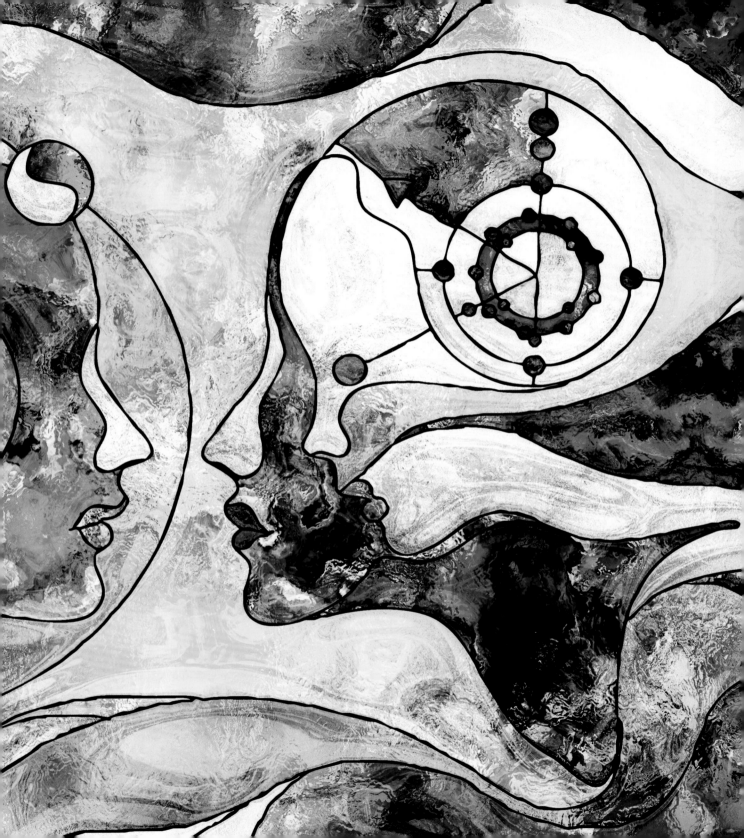

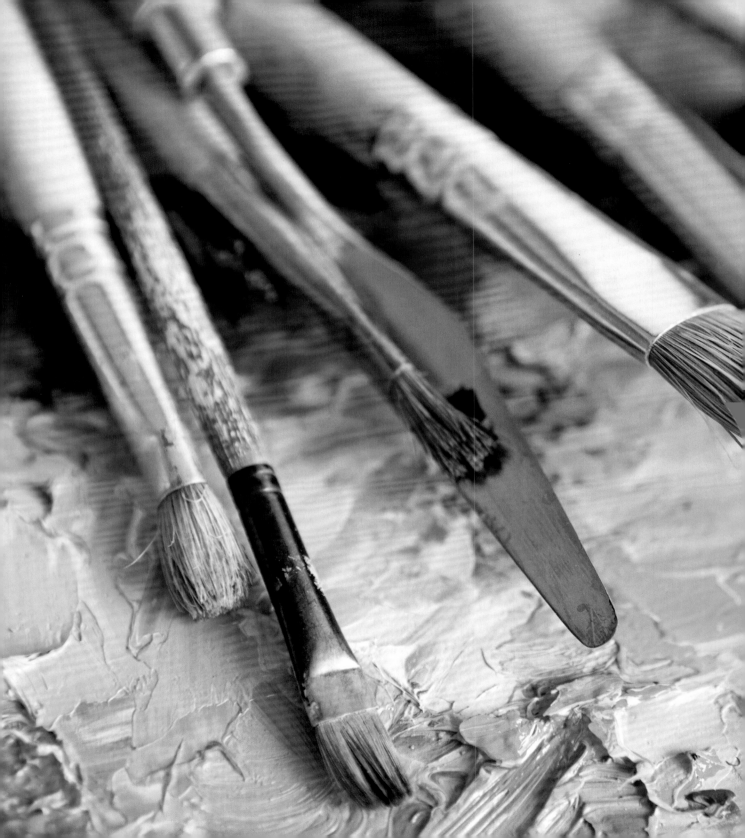

Associated with the nurturing energies of Cancer and the Moon. This is the house of your private life, domestic situations, tribes and groups that are in effect part of your extended family. This zone represents your parents, the mother in particular, and their influence. It also covers our past and ancestral roots as well as things that are hidden (emotionally or physically). The fourth house includes personal security.

The Fifth House

Main theme:
Creativity and pleasure – 'Let's go out to play.'

Associated with the creative energies of Leo and the Sun. This is the house of one's heart, of personal passions such as hobbies and sport, and the interests that lead to art or self-expressive work. The fifth house also covers procreation, one's own children (if any), fertility, leisure, recreational activities, romance and all things fun.

The Sixth House

Main theme:
Work, health and service – 'I am at your service.'

Associated with the practical energies of Virgo and Mercury. This is the house of daily activities, dedication to tasks, the people in your care, personal

wellbeing, illness, routine tasks and how we deal with trauma. Health, diet, nutrition, exercise and self-improvement are also included in this house.

The Seventh House

Main theme:

Relationships – 'It's not all about me.'

Associated with the cooperative energies of Libra and Venus. This is the house of all kinds of partnership – intimate and professional or business. It includes one's partner or lover, contracts involving partnership, negotiations, diplomacy, close personal friends and harmony between people. It is also the house of open enemies and lawsuits.

The Eighth House

Main theme:

Transformation – 'Change is as good as a rest.'

Associated with the healing energies of Scorpio and Pluto (and Mars). This is the house of death but also of renewal, regeneration and transformation. It covers financial themes, especially taxes, shared property and wealth (such as in marriage), and money held in a bank. Generally, the eighth house is the zone of finding self-empowerment and facing major problems.

The Ninth House

Main theme:

Growth and faith – 'What is my next challenge?'

Associated with the enlightening energies of Sagittarius and Jupiter. This is the house of philosophy, long-distance travel, church, foreign

interests, higher education and new personal territory, which includes taking risks for advancement. The ninth house also covers the justice system, long-term commitments or study and doing things on faith.

The Tenth house

Main theme: Life objectives or career – 'Aim high.'

Associated with the ambitious energies of Capricorn and Saturn. This is the house of status, responsibility, fame, honours and the father. The tenth house is

connected to the Midheaven point (*see* page 68) and has to do with advancement and the strategies adopted to get you to where you want to be in life. Also covers governments and royalty.

The Eleventh house

Main theme:
Friends and groups – 'Join me on a demo.'

Associated with the campaigning energies of Aquarius and Uranus. This is the house of collective activity, professional alliances and allies. It also includes ambitions outside of one's career – such as to improve the lot of humanity – and the gains from business. Covers networking, charity work and deciding who is useful to you and who is not.

The Twelfth House

Main theme: Spirituality and consequences – 'Who knows what lies beyond?'

Associated with the soulful energies of Pisces and Neptune. This is the house of mystery that includes dreams, secrets, psychology, hidden enemies and all things of another dimension, such as the paranormal. It also covers confined places (such as hospitals and jails), healing, acting behind the scenes of events and secretive or veiled activities.

Stay Healthy

Sagittarius
Constant challenges to feel totally alive.

Capricorn
Wining and dining offer the best relaxation.

Aquarius
An online debate for a cathartic battle.

Pisces
A sanctuary to develop inner peace.

'Each one of our lives comes with
a purpose, and it's not from the ego that
we get that dream. It's from the soul, and
that is imprinted on the sky. Your astrological
chart is that map that decodes the dream that your
soul has or the dream that the universe has for you.'

The Planets

The word 'planet' means a celestial body in our solar system that moves through the zodiac. Here are 10 main planets in the horoscope, each representing different life themes. This includes the Sun and Moon, which in astrology are also referred to as planets.

'Astrology isn't fortune-telling, nor do astrologers speak of life being fated. As agents of free will, we always have a choice.'

Susan Miller, American astrologer

The symbolism of the planets comes from ancient beliefs and religions through different ages. For instance, Mars became the 'God of War' because it is red – a colour associated with anger and violence. Venus is linked to beautiful things because it sparkles brightly like a jewel. Jupiter represents growth because it is enormous.

What the Planets Symbolize

 THE SUN

Character and identity: Its zodiac sign and chart house reveal what kind of person you are and how you tackle such experiences as work, love or struggle. It spends a month in each sign, taking a year to complete the zodiac, from Aries to Pisces. The Sun rules (or is associated with) Leo and the fifth house.

US astrologer Grant Lewi: 'The Sun indicates the psychological bias which will dominate your actions.'

 THE MOON

Emotions and reflexes: Its zodiac sign and chart house reveal how we respond to situations, the depth of our intuition and the power of our dreams. It moves quickly, spending about two and a half days in each sign, taking

about 28 days to complete the zodiac. The Moon rules Cancer and is associated with the fourth house.

Astrologer Susan Miller of astrozone.com:
'The Moon drives your deepest feelings, the fine-tuning of your character, your instinct and intuition.'

MERCURY

Communications: Its zodiac sign and chart house reveal how we share information with other people. The 'mind planet' governs how we make sense of

'You can change what is written in your horoscope. By acting at your lowest good, you can turn an otherwise very good horoscope into a very challenging life. But by acting by your highest good you can definitely transform an astrological lemon of a chart into terrestrial lemonade. The sugar is consciousness.'

Alan Oken, American astrologer and author

the world. It stays in a sign for between 15 and 60 days and completes the zodiac in just under a year. Mercury rules Gemini and Virgo, and is associated with the third and sixth houses.

Astrologer Alice Sparkly Cat: 'How Mercury behaves might just help you better harness your voice to its greatest abilities.'

VENUS

Relationships and money: Its zodiac sign and chart house reveal how we deal with love and the things we value. This is a social planet, to do with friendships and other attachments. It stays in a sign for up five weeks and completes the zodiac in about one year. Venus rules Taurus and Libra and is associated with the second and seventh houses.

UK astrologer Deborah Houlding: 'Venus seeks luxury and all the pleasant things we associate with self-indulgence.'

MARS

Energy and drive: Its zodiac sign and chart house reveal how determined we are and how we express our anger. The planet also rules war, competitive sports and physical prowess. It stays in a sign for up to seven weeks and completes the zodiac in about two years. Mars rules Aries and Scorpio and is associated with the first and eighth houses.

Astrologer Lisa Stardust: 'Mars shows how you take action and argue and shows your sexual inclinations.'

 JUPITER

Luck and opportunity.: Its zodiac sign and chart house reveal how easy life will be and the extent to which we are prepared to take risks for personal expansion. Jupiter stays in a sign for about a year and completes the zodiac in 12 years. Jupiter rules Sagittarius and is associated with the ninth house.

Astrologer Cate East: 'Jupiter takes chances. The more chances one seems to take, the more likely one can find opportunities.'

SATURN

Responsibility and ambition: Its zodiac sign and chart house reveal how we deal with duties, restrictions, obligations and status. It is often called life's 'taskmaster' and 'timekeeper', imposing discipline to achieve success. The planet spends between two and three years in a sign, rules Capricorn and is associated with the tenth house.

UK astrologer Russell Grant: 'Saturn encourages you to let go of anything in your life that has gone stale.'

URANUS

Independence and originality: Its zodiac sign and chart house reveal how ready we are to challenge authority if we have a vision of how things ought to be. Planet of sudden inspiration, eccentricity or unorthodoxy. The planet spends about seven years in a sign, rules Aquarius and is associated with the eleventh house.

Astrologer Molly Hall: 'Uranus is the cosmic alarm clock, and big shocks and surprises often match up with this planet's doing.'

NEPTUNE

Imagination and spirituality: Its zodiac sign and chart house reveal how receptive we are to inspiration and dreams, and whether we can tell the difference between fact and fiction. It also rules all types of illusion. The planet stays in a sign for up to 12 years, rules Pisces and is associated with the twelfth house.

Astrology site cafeastrology.com: 'Neptune rules all things subtle. A youthful spirit characterizes those with a strong placement of Neptune.'

PLUTO

Death and transformation: Its zodiac sign and chart house reveal how we handle major challenges and adapt to new life phases. This is the planet of self-empowerment and signifies what we must experience in order to grow. The planet stays in a sign for up to 15 years, co-rules Scorpio and is associated with the eighth house.

The AstroTwins (Elle.com): 'Pluto shows the thing you have to keep on sacrificing in order to do your most important soul growth!'

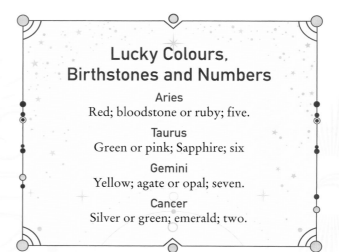

Lucky Colours, Birthstones and Numbers

Aries
Red; bloodstone or ruby; five.

Taurus
Green or pink; Sapphire; six.

Gemini
Yellow; agate or opal; seven.

Cancer
Silver or green; emerald; two.

'Astrology is currently enjoying a broad cultural acceptance that hasn't been seen since the nineteen-seventies.'

The New Yorker

Personality and Career

If your birth time is known, the horoscope can tell what kind of personality you have and what sort of work would suit you best. To do this we examine the Ascendant and Midheaven points.

It is easy to discover which signs your Ascendant and Midheaven (often shortened to AC and MC) are in. Just enter all your birth data into an astrology app or into a free website like Astrodienst at astro.com and you will find out in seconds.

Ascendant: Our Personality

The personality is the way we come across to people. It is the social mask we wear and is not to be confused with your real character – represented by the Sun sign. So, to clarify, in most people's charts, the Sun (character) and Ascendant (personality) are in different signs. This is why many people turn out to be different once you have got to know them better. But if the Sun and Ascendant are in the same sign, the person presents themselves as they really are.

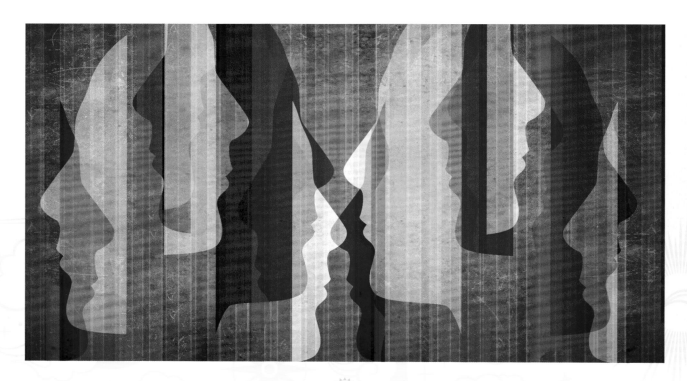

If they'd given me half
an Oscar, I would have thrown
it back in their faces. You see,
I'm an Aries. I never lose.

Bette Davis, American actor

Aries Ascendant: Bold, sharp, impatient, direct and decisive. No time to waste. Capable of being cutting in their words.

Taurus Ascendant: Slightly reserved, patient, sensual and methodical. Not one to rush. Seeks comfort and security.

Gemini Ascendant: Chatty, curious, gossipy, well informed and easily bored. Gets to the point quickly. Fickleness can be a problem.

Cancer Ascendant: Caring, sensitive, warm, watchful and shy at first. Never forgets a slight or a compliment. Famous for a long memory.

Leo Ascendant: Striking, theatrical, noisy, boastful and very warm. Always makes an impact. Capable of great courage.

Virgo Ascendant: Reserved, friendly, analytical, nervy and modest. Notices all the little things. A sign of remarkable kindness and quirkiness.

Libra Ascendant: Charming, conversational, stylish, embracing and conciliatory. Tries to keep the peace. Often disguises true feelings.

Scorpio Ascendant: Magnetic, brooding, shrewd, secretive and intense. Tells the truth – eventually. Possesses immense charisma.

Sagittarius Ascendant: Scintillating, sociable, forthright, knowledgeable and brutally direct. Larger than life. Always seeking fresh fields.

Capricorn Ascendant: Studious, focused, no-nonsense, drily witty and down to earth. Always aims high. Born to lead and manage.

☀ **Aquarius Ascendant**: Shocking, intellectual, eccentric, popular and rebellious. Nothing is sacred. Works best as a singleton within groups.

☀ **Pisces Ascendant**: Dreamy, mysterious, vague at times, insightful and empathetic. Can spot a trend a mile off. Never to be underestimated.

Midheaven: Our Path

The Midheaven (marking the chart point of the midday Sun) symbolizes your life direction or career and is found at the top of your horoscope. The Midheaven describes the sort of energies best suited for certain occupations and is found in one of the 12 zodiac signs.

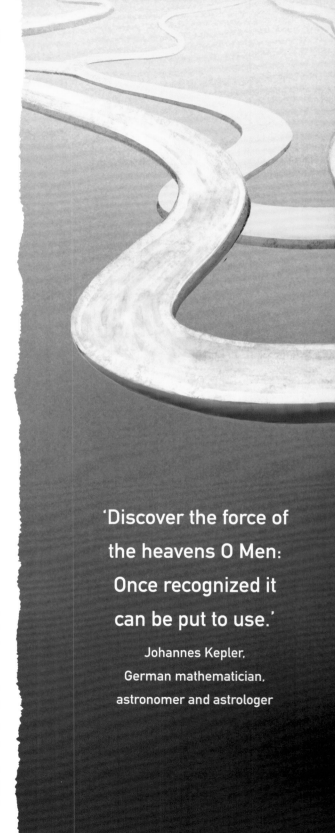

'Discover the force of the heavens O Men: Once recognized it can be put to use.'

Johannes Kepler, German mathematician, astronomer and astrologer

☀ **Aries Midheaven:** Any work where independence or personal initiative are encouraged. Self-employment is best. Or being the boss.

☀ **Taurus Midheaven:** Creative jobs are perfect where beauty or harmony is the theme. Music, fashion, gardening or style-related work would suit.

'Heaven sends down its good and evil symbols and wise men act accordingly.'

Confucius

☀ **Gemini Midheaven**: Anything involving writing, speaking or marketing is ideal. A buzzy environment such as in journalism, sales or marketing.

☀ **Cancer Midheaven**: Compassion, caring and nurturing are strong points; human resources or hospitality would be good matches. Would also make a great therapist.

☀ **Leo Midheaven**: There is a strong need to self-express, so acting or running any kind of organization is fulfilling. Government and teaching are also appropriate.

☀ **Virgo Midheaven**: Health, hygiene and analysis are the strong points. Nursing, the medical profession, accountancy, writing and editing should be considered.

☀ **Libra Midheaven**: There is a desire to resolve disputes or act as an intermediary. The legal profession and the arts may appeal.

☀ **Scorpio Midheaven**: With an instinct to delve and discover, a career in the police force, the law or psychotherapy would suit.

☀ **Sagittarius Midheaven**: Acquiring knowledge and seeking adventure are primary needs. Lecturing, religious posts or the travel sector are possible.

☀ **Capricorn Midheaven**: High ambition suits any profession which offers rich rewards for hard work, such as law, medicine, architecture or politics.

☀ **Aquarius Midheaven**: Humanitarian instincts suggest charity work. Technical wizardry opens up a world of computing and online retail.

☀ **Pisces Midheaven**: Artistic and intuitive gifts can be channelled into the creative arts, spiritual therapies or work requiring an understanding of trends.

Lucky Colours, Birthstones and Numbers

Leo
Orange or gold; onyx; 19.

Virgo
Brown or grey; carnelian; seven.

Libra
Pink; peridot; three.

Scorpio
Black; aquamarine; four.

The Aspects

To help us understand what a horoscope is saying, we measure the distance between planets and points by the number of degrees between them. These distances are called 'aspects' and can be automatically calculated by computers. There is no need to do any counting!

Each of these aspects tells us if a planet is helped or challenged by another planet, and whether there is good or bad news to report. Computer-created horoscopes automatically show different-coloured lines between two (or more) planets to indicate the type of aspect involved.

'In astrology…one has to…step beyond the visible world of matter.'

H. P. Blavatsky, co-founder, Theosophical Society

How Are the Aspects Created?

An aspect is created when two or more planets are together on one spot in a chart or are on the same degree but in different signs. For instance, Mars may be at three degrees Capricorn opposite Uranus at three degrees Cancer – this is called an 'opposition'. There are five major aspects to look out for. Here is a brief guide to them along with celebrity examples and the usual colour of the aspect lines.

CONJUNCTION

Two planets sit on the same degree or are very close together in the chart. The energies of both planets are blended, and this is usually regarded as a positive thing. But not always. Sometimes the two planets may be up to eight degrees apart, but this is still treated as a conjunction, and a red line shows they are linked.

 **SEXTILE**

Two planets sit 60 degrees apart in the chart, two signs away from each other. This is indicated by a short blue line. A sextile is a very positive energy and suggests opportunity and harmony, depending on which planets are linked in this way.

Marilyn Monroe

In her horoscope, Venus (beauty and tastes) is sextile her Jupiter (growth and expansion) and Moon (emotional nature). The sextile – which means Venus is about 60 degrees away from the other two planets – represents opportunity. The chart shows that her looks would be important in her success.

 ## SQUARE

Two planets sit 90 degrees apart, three signs separating them.
The aspect line is short and red. This is a challenging aspect,
which suggests that obstacles or disappointments may have to
be faced, depending on which planets are involved. However,
the square can strengthen the character through determination,
facing reality or side-stepping a foreseeable problem.

Mother Teresa (Saint Teresa of Calcutta)

In her horoscope Mercury is square Pluto,
which means her thinking and motivation
(Mercury) were greatly affected by very difficult
and dark situations (Pluto). A Roman Catholic
nun, she dedicated her life to helping the very
sick and poor in India, saving countless lives,
despite criticism of her approach.

TRINE

Two planets sit 120 degrees apart, four signs separating them. The long aspect line is coloured blue. This is a very positive aspect, which indicates harmonious energies and is favourable, depending on the planets involved. However, there is a risk of complacency if life is taken for granted.

Elvis Presley

In his horoscope, Neptune (inspiration) at the top of his chart is trine his Sun (identity), Mercury (mind and words) and Venus (personal tastes) in Capricorn. This trine – that is, Neptune is about 120 degrees away from the other three planets – reflects a highly artistic individual.

OPPOSITION

Two planets sit opposite each other, 180 degrees apart, six signs separating them. A long red line across the chart denotes the aspect. This is a challenging aspect, which means that there is a need to find a compromise, depending on which planets are involved. The opposition can be helpful only if you do not adopt a dogmatic or fixed attitude.

John Lennon

In his horoscope, Mercury (mind and words) opposes his Jupiter (growth) and Saturn (restriction, responsibilities). The opposition – which means Mercury is about 180 degrees away from the other two planets – symbolizes tension. The chart shows Lennon was open-minded but would have had to resist attempts to control him.

Flexibility in Creating an Aspect

We saw that generally an exact aspect is where two planets are on the same degree in a sign or on the same degree in different signs. But an aspect does not have to be this exact. Astrologers allow up to eight degrees either side of an aspect for it to be created.

For example, if your Sun is at 10 degrees Gemini and is square Neptune at two degrees (or even 18 degrees) Virgo, this is still recognized as a square. This allowance is called an 'orb'. You will hear astrologers say that an aspect is 'within orb'. They mean that the aspect is not exact but still within range to be created.

Four Minor Aspects

There are other aspects and here is a brief introduction to four of them.

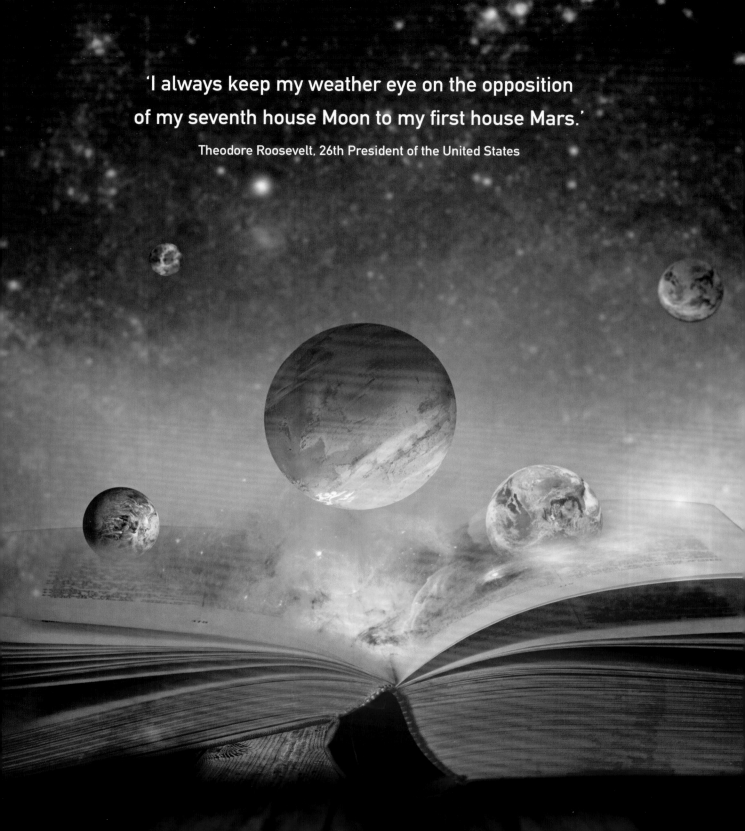

'I always keep my weather eye on the opposition of my seventh house Moon to my first house Mars.'

Theodore Roosevelt, 26th President of the United States

SEMI-SEXTILE

Two planets are 30 degrees apart, one sign separating them. This is helpful provided boundaries are respected.

 ## SEMI-SQUARE

Two planets are 45 degrees apart, one and a half signs separating them. Minor obstacles are indicated.

 ## SESQUIQUADRATE

Two planets 135 degrees apart, four and a half signs separating them. Suppressed problems need to be addressed.

 ## QUINCUNX (OR INCONJUNCT)

Two planets are 150 degrees apart, five signs separating them. Indicates incompatibilities. The 'live and let live' approach is advised.

Lucky Colours, Birthstones and Numbers

Sagittarius
Purple or light blue; topaz; six.

Capricorn
Black or grey; ruby or black jade; four.

Aquarius
Blue or bronze; garnet; 22.

Pisces
Light green or white; amethyst; 11.

'As astrologers we need to be able to see above what is being played out in the present, have learned wisdom from the past, and still look bravely toward the future.'

Michael Lutin, American astrologer and author

How to Read a Horoscope

A horoscope chart can be used to do many different things – analyse a person's life and character, make forecasts, assess whether two people in a relationship are right for each other, and many other things besides.

Setting up the Horoscope

The best place to start is with your own birth horoscope. Who knows you better than you? You can create your horoscope on one of many reliable astrology websites or phone apps.

For my guide to the best free ones, turn to the Astrology Online section towards the end of this book (*see* page 120). All you need do is enter your birth data, click a button and an instant horoscope is created.

What Do Astrologers Look for in a Chart?

Your Sun sign is only one part of a horoscope. All 10 planets represent you in various ways and are likely to be placed in different signs and houses – and these positions help to build a three-dimensional profile of you.

'The essential purpose of astrology is not so much to tell us what we will meet on our road as it is to suggest how to meet it – and the basic reason for the meeting.'

Dane Rudhyar, French author, composer and astrologer

Look back at the sections in this book on planets and signs for their meaning and refamiliarize yourself with the symbols. This section draws together all the things we have talked about already. There are six basic steps for chart interpretation.

Step 1: Interpreting the Planets

Start by looking to see which sign your Sun is in. Then see where your Moon is – if it is in a different sign, this will add another layer of understanding. Then discover which sign your Ascendant is in – if it is different from your Sun sign, this too will modify character.

My Horoscope as an Example

My Sun (character) is in Gemini. I am curious, restless and communicative – I write and edit for a living. My Ascendant (personality) is in Aquarius. This modifies my Gemini nature by drawing me to unusual subjects (such as astrology) and adding unpredictability. My Moon (emotions) is in Pisces. This modifies me even further by making me highly sensitive and a lot more intuitive than the 'average' Gemini who tends to be mentally driven.

So, already, you see I am not a 'typical' Gemini, because I am rather offbeat and hyper-sensitive. In fact, most people are not entirely typical of their Sun signs.

Now Look at the Other Planets

Discover which signs your other eight planets are in. Some may share a sign or be in other parts of the chart. For instance, Meryl Streep has her Sun, Venus and Uranus in Cancer, which heightens her sensitivity as an actress.

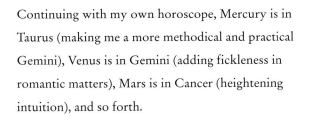

Continuing with my own horoscope, Mercury is in Taurus (making me a more methodical and practical Gemini), Venus is in Gemini (adding fickleness in romantic matters), Mars is in Cancer (heightening intuition), and so forth.

There are many astrological websites which give free interpretations of planets-in-signs – look them up. Gradually you will build a profile of yourself by blending the different perspectives of each planet.

Step 2: Interpreting Your Chart Houses

The planets sit not just in zodiac signs but also in the 12 houses, and each house as we have seen represents a different area of life. This adds yet another layer of meaning and understanding.

One or more planets can occupy one house. For instance, in Tom Hanks' horoscope, Sun, Venus and Mercury are in his tenth house (career), explaining his great success as an actor.

Blend the planet(s) themes with the house themes. For instance, Hanks' Saturn (rigour) in Scorpio (depth) is in his third house (communications), accounting for his disciplined image and rigorous approach to scripts.

Birth Time and the Houses

Where your planets sit in the houses depends on your time of birth, automatically calculated by computers. But what if you do not know your birth time? In this case, astrologers set the chart for midnight or midday, and you can do this also. This creates a chart with planets in assigned houses.

'The celestial bodies are the cause of all that takes place in the sublunar world.'

St Thomas Aquinas

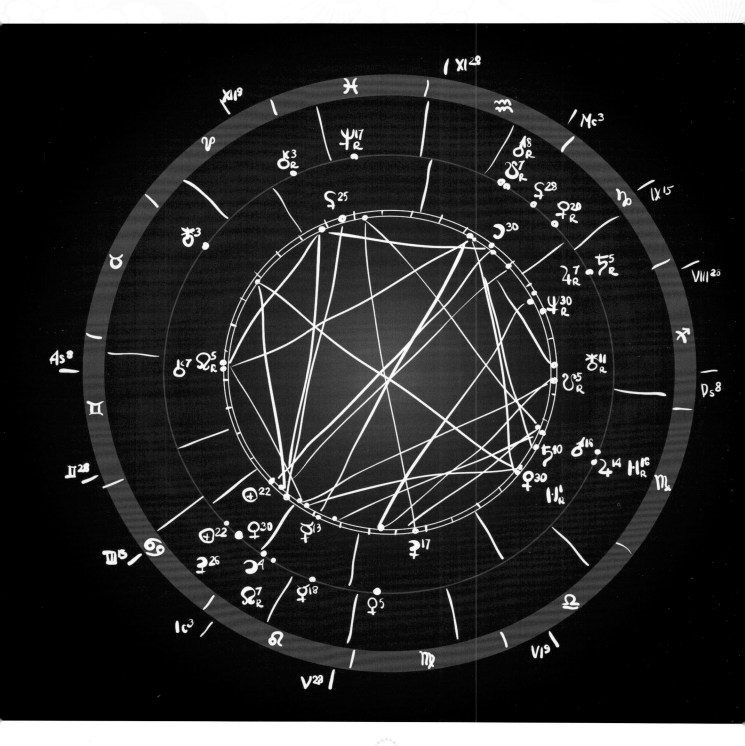

Step 3: Interpreting Aspects

Once you have built a basic profile of yourself from the planets, signs and houses, you turn to whether the planets are linked to each other by aspect. For instance, if your Mars is 90 degrees (or so) from Venus, this is a square.

As we saw earlier, aspects in a computer-created chart are shown by coloured lines (*see* page 72). Each aspect is symbolic and tells you whether the planets involved are helped or challenged.

In Will Smith's horoscope, a short red line links his Moon and Neptune in a conjunction, indicating an imaginative nature (Moon) and involvement in movies, through the symbolism of 'optical illusion' (Neptune). In Madonna's chart, a longer red line links Mars and Uranus (a square), suggesting a highly restless temperament.

Step 4: Interpreting Aspect Patterns and Shapes

Sometimes three or more planets create 'aspect patterns'. The most common one is a T-square which is triangular and formed of one opposition between two planets both linked to a third (apex) planet by sextiles. This symbolizes that a problem can be solved by focusing on the themes of the third planet.

'Chart shapes' also reveal things about you. One is called a Seesaw, where the planets are bunched into two opposing groups. This indicates a life where finding balance is a major topic. If your planets are scattered evenly around the chart (a Splash), you are an adaptable person likely to have a life of unusual variety.

Step 5: Interpreting Chart Hemispheres

You can tell a lot about a person by how the planets are scattered around the horoscope. If you have a majority of planets in one of the four hemispheres, the following character traits are revealed.

☀ **Eastern hemisphere (left-hand half of the chart):**
A highly independent person guided by their
own judgments.

☀ **Western hemisphere (right-hand half of the chart):**
A people pleaser who works best in groups.

☀ **Southern hemisphere (top half of the chart):** A lot of
social and professional engagement with the world.

☀ **Northern hemisphere (bottom half of the chart):**
A tendency to preoccupation with the
self and private life.

Step 6: The Moon's Nodes: Life Purpose

The two nodes are to do with the Moon's movements
and are important. They are always in opposition to
each other and symbolize the overall purpose of your
life, depending on which sign and house they appear in.

 SOUTH NODE

This represents the instincts and talents you are born with.

 NORTH NODE

Also called the destiny point, this represents the
kind of challenges you may face to find fulfilment or
greater inner balance.

In Winston Churchill's chart, South Node is in Libra
(peace) and North Node is in Aries (war). This describes

'Perhaps there is a pattern
set up in the heavens
for one who desires to
see it, and having seen it,
to find one in himself.'

Plato, Ancient Greek philosopher

a life based on achieving harmony but warns that conflict must be faced to preserve harmony.

Three Useful Things to Remember

1 **Study the charts of celebrities or notable people**

In addition to studying your own chart, it is great fun to look at the charts of famous people. In the Astrology Online section (*see* page 120), I list websites and phone apps which publish celebrity horoscopes along with analyses.

Do not be put off if the different chart perspectives seem confusing at first. We have all been there! Gradually you will get used to thinking like an astrologer as you associate the chart symbols with what you know about the famous individual.

2 **Make notes as you analyse charts**

List where the 12 planets are in the signs and houses. This is the basis of your understanding of a horoscope. Writing things down will help you remember the meanings of symbols and encourage you not to rush.

3 **Use online searches to deepen your knowledge**

If, say, Moon is trine Sun and you are unsure what this means, many online search engines (such as Google) can be used to locate websites or apps for answers.

'It's common knowledge that a large percentage of Wall Street brokers use astrology.'

Donald T. Regan, Secretary of the Treasury and the White House Chief of Staff

The People We Find Attractive

Aries
Drawn to Librans because they create beauty.

Taurus
Intrigued by Scorpios because
they are for ever obsessing.

Gemini
Stunned by Sagittarians because
they speak the truth.

Cancer
Awed by Capricorns because of their ambition.

Charts of Famous People

One of the best ways to learn how astrology works is to examine the charts of the famous. You can link your chart observations with what you know about the person. Here we look, briefly and selectively, at the horoscopes (charts shown) of three prominent personalities.

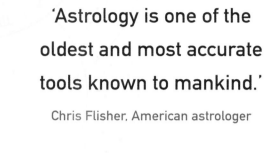

'Astrology is one of the oldest and most accurate tools known to mankind.'

Chris Flisher, American astrologer

Horoscope of Diana, Princess of Wales

Sun in Cancer in the Seventh House

Cancer is the sign of the mother and nurturer, and the seventh house is the zone of friends and partners. This immediately tells us that Diana had a pronounced caring disposition (Cancer) and a natural tendency to charm and please people (the seventh house). As we know, Diana was a hugely popular British royal and very loving to her two sons, William and Harry.

Moon in Aquarius in the Third House Opposite Uranus

Emotionally (Moon), Diana could reach out to people through humanitarian interests (Aquarius) and communicate with many different kinds of people (third house). One of her numerous campaigns was against the use of land mines.

Diana, Princess of Wales Natal Chart

1 Jul 1961, Sat • 19:45 BST -1:00 • Sandringham • 52°N50' 000°E30' • Geocentric • Tropical • Equal • Mean Node

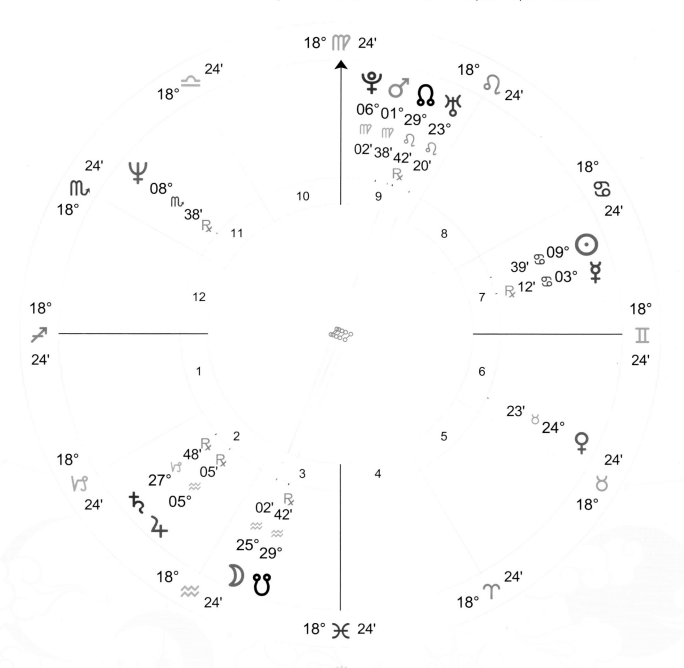

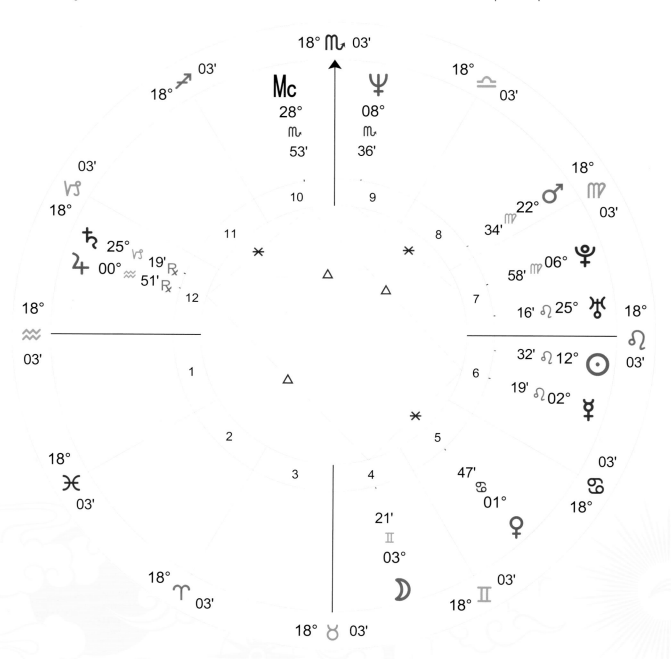

Barack Obama Natal Chart

4 Aug 1961, Fri • 19:24 AHST +10:00 • Honolulu, Hawaii • 21°N18'25" 157°W51'30" Geocentric • Tropical • Equal • Mean Node

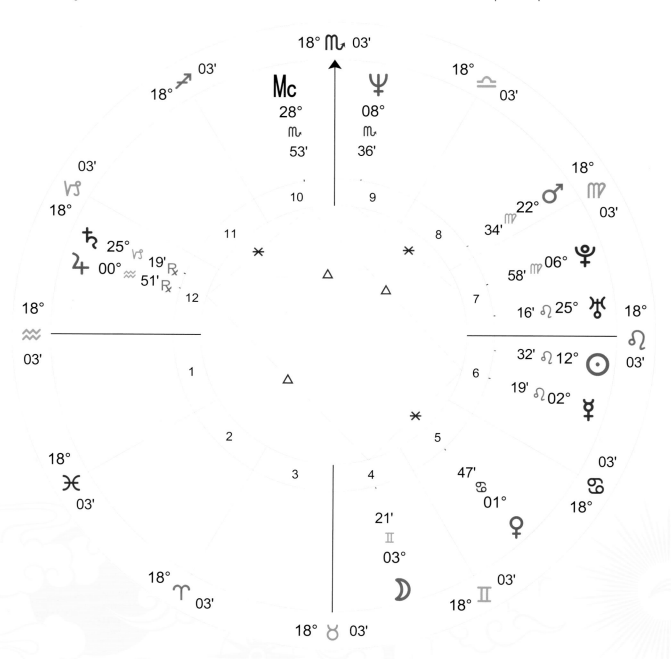

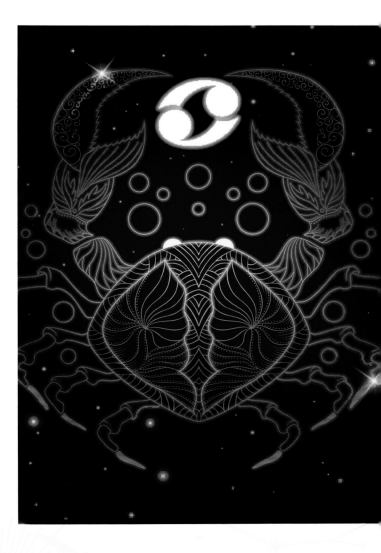

Her families (Moon) of origin and through marriage to Prince Charles tended to be unstable (Uranus in opposition to Moon). She could be emotionally erratic and was given to displays of temper and frustration (Uranus in Leo).

Ascendant in Sagittarius, Chart Ruler Jupiter in the Second House

Her personal image was sparkling, jovial, expansive and forthright (Sagittarius). The planet that rules Sagittarius and therefore the chart itself is Jupiter, and Diana's Jupiter is in Aquarius. Humanitarian campaigns (Aquarius) are assured success by her benevolence (Jupiter), driven by strong ethical concerns (second house). Jupiter in the second house (income and assets) can also be a sign of wealth.

Horoscope of Barack Obama, 44th US President

Sun, Mercury, Uranus in Leo, Sixth to Seventh Houses

Note how well represented Leo is in this chart, indicating a passionate and resolute man. The house positions of these planets tell us he is oriented to protect the vulnerable (sixth) and works through charm and negotiation (seventh).

Many Trine and Sextile Aspects

Two such aspects are Mars to Jupiter and Mercury to Moon. This tells us that he has a high likelihood

'The two most important positions in any natal chart, after the Sun sign, are the Ascendant and the Moon sign.'

Linda Goodman, American astrologer and poet

of success in life, because so many of his planets and points are in harmony with each other. There are challenging aspects (not shown) in his chart, but he is likely to overcome them.

A Very 'Fixed' Chart

Many of Obama's planets and points are in the fixed signs of Taurus, Leo, Scorpio and Aquarius. This bestows a very determined nature, which is not easily deflected from a course of action, and often indicates a self-composed character, something noted in many media profiles.

Aquarius Ascendant

With his Sun in Leo, Obama was born to shine. But with Aquarius rising, he is also capable of surprise moves that no one sees coming. One example is his very rapid rise to power after his surprise victory over Hillary Clinton in 2008 for the Democratic nomination.

Britney Spears, 'Princess of Pop'

Venus in Capricorn in the Fourth House Square Pluto and Saturn in Libra in the First House

This aspect reveals problems to do with family relationships (Venus in the fourth house) and authority figures (Saturn). As the world knows, following a high-profile campaign, she was released from a court-ordered conservatorship in late 2021, which had placed much control over her life in the hands of other people.

The square aspect tells us of the personal challenges she faces to find her independence. She can achieve this, but only through determination.

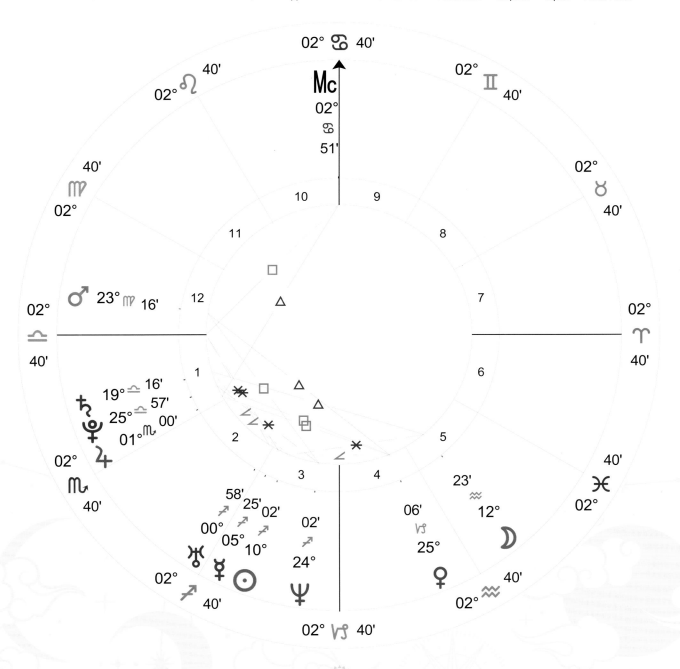

Britney Spears Natal Chart

2 Dec 1981, Wed • 01:30 CST +6:00 • McComb, Mississippi • 31°N14'37" 090°W27'11" • Geocentric • Tropical • Equal • Mean Node

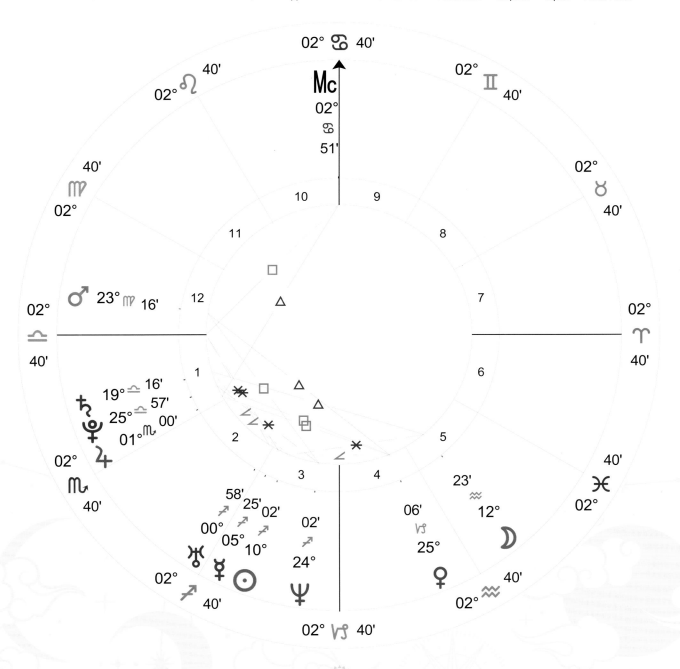

'I was born under the sign of Saturn – the planet of the slowest revolution, the star of hesitation and delay.'

Walter Benjamin, German philosopher

A Bowl Chart Led by Mars in the Twelfth House

The planets only occupy about one half of the chart, which makes this a Bowl horoscope. This is another indication of the need to find balance in her life. With Mars ('God of War') in Virgo 'leading' the Bowl, this is another indication that Spears must fight for what she values.

Four Planets in Sagittarius with Libra Ascendant

The powerful fire energy of Sagittarius gives Spears immense joie de vivre, helping her to overcome problems and find huge success. Her Libra Ascendant accentuates personal beauty and charm, disguising a very robust nature (Sagittarius).

The People We Find Attractive

Leo
Drawn to Aquarians because
of their unpredictability.

Virgo
Intrigued by Pisceans because they
rise above mundane matters.

Libra
Stunned by Arians because they
get things done fast.

Scorpio
Awed by Taureans because they
are so down to earth.

Forecasting

Astrologers can make specific predictions and general forecasts by examining the birth horoscope of a person, country and business, or any kind of situation, such as the future of a relationship.

The horoscope is like a time machine which can look back to the past, to discover what happened, and forwards to the future, to discover what will happen. Good astrologers can even tell you what is happening in the present. Later in this section we shall look at some famous examples of successful forecasts.

> 'Astrology is like a weather report; it tells you what conditions you're likely to face in the future. If the weatherman says it's probably going to rain, you bring an umbrella. If you follow that advice, you won't get wet.'
>
> Lee Goldberg, American meteorologist

Where Do We Start to Make a Forecast?

The main means of forecasting involves looking at the 'transits'. These are the movements of the 10 planets in the horoscope for any given moment, such as in the present or future. Transiting planets are constantly moving, unlike the planets in your birth chart, which do not move at all.

Astrology software programs instantly tell you where the transits are in the zodiac. But you can also find out by consulting a book called an ephemeris. This is like a railway timetable, which shows the position of all the planets in the zodiac at any time in the past, present and future.

For instance, reading my own ephemeris, I can tell you that on 5 January 2045 transiting Saturn will be in the eighth degree of Sagittarius, while transiting Pluto will be in the second degree of Pisces.

How Do I Use the Transits?

To make a forecast you first create two charts – one is the birth chart (perhaps yours), and the other is the transits chart. The transits chart will be placed on the outside of the birth chart. Software programs do this automatically.

The purpose of doing this is to discover what aspects are made (if any) between the transiting planets and your birth planets. For example, what if transiting Saturn is in conjunction with your Sun six months from now? That could indicate a time of very hard work or a new responsibility. If, say, transiting Neptune is in an opposition to your birth Venus a year from now, that could mean that a relationship is due to enter a confusing time.

How Can I Interpret the Transits Quickly?

When you see an aspect between a transiting planet and a birth planet (for instance, transiting Mars trine birth Jupiter), use an online search engine to find astrology websites that offer interpretations. Remember to write 'transiting Mars trine Jupiter' in the search box. Do not fall into the trap of assuming the worst if an interpretation seems gloomy. No astrologer can forecast precisely how an aspect will show itself in real life; what might look like a future problem could well turn out to be a chance to do something new.

Synastry: 'Will My Relationship Work Out?'

This technique compares the charts of two people to work out whether they are compatible. The more harmonious the aspects (sextiles, trines, conjunctions) between the planets of the two charts, the more likely it is that the relationship will prove long-lasting.

To do the synastry in an astrology software program, you create the two birth charts and then press the synastry option. You will then see what is called a 'biwheel', which is the two charts together, one on the outside of the other.

What Are You Looking for in Synastry?

If Person A's Venus is conjunct (i.e. 'in conjunction with') Person B's Venus, this is a strong sign of compatibility. If square, then friction is likely. Look at all the aspects to assess the overall condition of the relationship.

In the synastry of Queen Elizabeth II and Prince Philip, her Venus is conjunct his Uranus, suggesting a powerful bond, but one that would have had to cope with his restlessness (Uranus).

In the synastry of Angelina Jolie and Brad Pitt, her Venus is opposite his Venus, which shows a need to find compromises if the bond is to work out. They divorced in 2019.

Other Predictive Techniques

Aside from the transits, astrologers have developed other ways of reading the future. Here is a brief guide to the main ones.

- ☀ **Solar returns:** This is also called your birthday chart. When the transiting Sun returns to the exact position of your birth Sun, this is a return; hence the saying, 'Many happy returns'. When the two Suns are together, the position of the other transiting planets in the return chart tells you what kind of year you are going to have.

☀ **Secondary progressions**: This is used mainly to indicate the 'mood' of the future and your personal development. This system converts each year of your life after birth into a day and each day is given one degree. So, if you are 40 years old, your progressed Sun will be 40 degrees away from your birth Sun.

☀ **Solar arc directions**: A specialized timing technique to discover when certain events will occur.

☀ **Horary**: A traditional technique that answers specific questions requiring a 'Yes' or a 'No' answer. The chart is created for the moment the question is posed to the astrologer.

☀ **Elections**: A system that identifies the perfect day in a horoscope to do something, such as to get married or start a business. A few years back I was asked to elect the perfect moment for the launch of a London nightclub. The club is still a great success.

'There is something out there. Astrology is like a game of chess with an invisible partner. We set out the board and the rules, make a move, and then find that the pieces are moving themselves, as if by an invisible hand.'

Noel Tyl, American astrologer

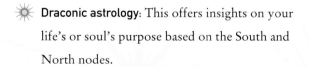 **Draconic astrology:** This offers insights on your life's or soul's purpose based on the South and North nodes.

Famous Forecasts in History That Proved True

The Great Fire of London of 1666

This disaster was forecast by the great English astrologer William Lilly (1602–1681) 14 years before the event. Parliament was so troubled by his accuracy that he was investigated on suspicion of arson. Fortunately, he was cleared.

The COVID-19 Pandemic

The French astrologer André Barbault (1921–2019) wrote in 2011: 'It may well be that we are seriously threatened by a new pandemic in 2020–21.' The COVID-19 pandemic started in early 2020.

US President Ronald Reagan and a Health Forecast

First Lady Nancy Reagan's personal astrologer Joan Quigley (1927–2014) foretold that President Ronald Reagan would require surgery in July 1985. This proved correct, when it was discovered he had cancer. Quigley was concerned about the timing of the operation and recommended 13 July at noon for success. This advice was followed and Reagan made a full recovery.

A Forecast of the 9/11 Attacks on US Soil

US astrologer Robert Zoller (1947–2020) foretold in 1999 that Osama bin Laden (leader of the terrorist group al-Qaeda) would launch an attack on the US in September 2001 at the time of the 'House of Bush' – a reference to President George W. Bush. The attacks occurred on 11 September 2001, during his presidency.

The People We Find Attractive

Sagittarius
Drawn to Geminis because of their conversation.

Capricorn
Intrigued by Cancerians because of their loyalty.

Aquarius
Stunned by Leos because of their passion.

Pisces
Awed by Virgos because they are so precise and analytical.

'Astrology reveals the will of the gods.'

Juvenal, Roman poet

Retrogrades

The Mercury retrograde fascinates a great number of people and is associated with things going wrong or haywire. It regularly trends on social media when the planet moves backwards in the sky. But is the retrograde all that it seems?

In fact, Mercury is not moving backwards at all. It just appears to be. It is an optical illusion due to the different speeds at which Earth and Mercury move in their orbits around the Sun.

At certain points in the year Earth 'passes' Mercury (like a fast car taking over a slower one), so that Mercury looks like it is moving backwards.

Do Other Planets Move Retrograde?

All the planets (except the Sun and Moon) go retrograde from time to time. The Mercury retrograde occurs three or four times a year and each retrograde lasts about three weeks. The Venus retrograde occurs every 18 months. Jupiter goes retrograde about every nine months. Once retrogrades are over, the planets move forward again through the zodiac.

> '**Retrograde Mercury is the only enemy writers have.**'
>
> Mitta Xinindlu, South African writer

Though retrogrades are 'illusions', bear in mind that astrologers are interested in what is seen in the sky

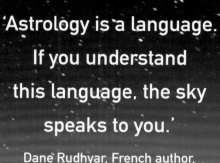

'Astrology is a language.
If you understand
this language, the sky
speaks to you.'

Dane Rudhyar, French author,
composer and astrologer

and attach meanings to what is apparent. They are generally not concerned with scientific explanations, even though they are aware of them.

The Symbolic Meaning of the Mercury Retrograde

In astrology Mercury represents communications, travel, contracts, mental processes, selling and buying, and so forth. When the planet moves retrograde, it is thought that there is a greater likelihood of disruption or unexpected delays if greater care is not taken. Imagine a car moving backwards – if you do not keep a watchful eye on the rear-view mirror, a calamity is likely to happen. The same kind of logic applies to the Mercury retrograde.

Things to Avoid During a Mercury Retrograde

- Signing contracts.
- Buying a property.
- Booking holidays.
- Assuming that a letter or email will arrive safely.
- Assuming that any message you send will not go to the wrong person.

Keep a diary during a retrograde and see whether you experience more disruption in your life than usual. Always test astrology and do not assume the worst.

The Venus Retrograde

Venus represents relationships, beauty, lifestyle and fashion. When the planet goes retrograde, usually for about six weeks, try to avoid starting a romantic relationship or having cosmetic surgery. This retrograde raises the chance of a former love, enemy, friend or colleague re-entering your life.

The Mars Retrograde

Mars has to do with our energy levels – or 'mojo' – so this retrograde (which occurs approximately every two years) is associated with lethargy, indifference and a lack of willpower. It may also be a period of physically slowing down, which may be a good thing if you need to recharge your batteries.

Other Retrogrades

Jupiter's retrograde lasts for a period of about four months, when it is wise to reflect on the wisdom of certain actions.

Saturn's retrograde lasts about one-third of the year, when it is wise to review how someone may be limiting your freedom.

The retrogrades of Uranus, Neptune and Pluto are lengthy and opinions differ on their symbolism.

Lucky Lunar Timings

Monthly New Moons

This is when the Sun and Moon are in conjunction and the Moon is invisible from Earth. It is a good time to start a relationship, business project, plan or to forgive someone.

Monthly Full Moons

When the Sun and Moon are in opposition, and the Moon shines brightly. A time to complete a project, end a poor relationship, tell someone what you feel or to 'harvest' something (crops or profits).

'The stars in the heavens sing a music if only we had ears to hear.'

Pythagoras, Ancient Greek mathematician

Astrology Online

Websites and phone apps have revolutionized astrology, providing free use of computer software programs that quickly create horoscope charts and interpretations. Here is a selection of the best.

Horoscope Creator Websites

astro-charts.com Very easy to use. Just click Create Chart for the birth data form. It also has a celebrity Sun sign feature.

astro.com Astrodienst is by far the largest of the astrology resource websites, with many free features. Most impressive is its astrology software that enables you to generate free horoscope charts, yours or anyone else's. Go to Extended Chart Selection to create a chart. Also has a free ephemeris covering 9000 years.

astrology.com.tr A simple-to-navigate site with chart creators that include various techniques such as solar returns and a Moon Phase Calculator.

alabe.com Astrolabe's best feature is the guide to understanding the chart symbols. This is a good site to visit once you have learnt a little more about astrology.

Website Astrology Guides

astrologyking.com Astrology King offers articulate and thorough interpretations of the aspects (natal and transits), each one of which includes a list of notable people who share the aspect in their birth charts. Ideal for familiarizing yourself with planetary symbolism.

cafeastrology.com Cafe Astrology has an impressive array of features that include readable explanations of

planets and points in signs and all the major aspects. Very useful to build up your knowledge of how to read a horoscope.

Celebrity Data Websites

astro.com/astro-databank A massive collection of astrological data on historical figures, celebrities and other famous people, with birth data, a short biography and horoscope. The site is part of Astrodienst.

astrotheme.com Free reports on celebrity charts along with a 'most viewed' list by visitors from the day before.

Astrology Phone Apps

TIMEPASSAGES

Download from the App Store/Google Play

Enter your birth data for a personalized dashboard that includes your horoscope and interpretations. Some other services are charged.

SANCTUARY

Download from App Store/Google Play

A mix of free and charged services. Free guides and personalized horoscope.

Astrology Software Programs

SOLAR FIRE

esotech.com.au

For Windows. Solar Fire is a world leader in astrology software programs.

ASTRO GOLD

astrogold.io

Available for iOS devices, including the iPhone, iPad and iPod touch, as well as for Mac desktops and laptops.

SIRIUS

astrosoftware.com/sirius.htm

For Windows. Easy to use and contains Astro-Databank celebrity birth data.

LUNA

lunaastrology.com

Cloud-based software that works on all devices – PC, Mac, Android, iPad, etc.

Further Resources

There are countless books and many good astrology schools, and here I select a few of them. For further advice on learning astrology, contact me via my website at victorolliver.co.uk

Books

What Astrology Is … and How to Use It,
by Bruce Scofield
A no-frills, fairly detailed introduction to astrology, which covers many techniques and offers a psychological approach in addition.

The Only Astrology Book You'll Ever Need,
by Joanna Martine Woolfolk
Bestselling and highly accessible guide, covering all the essential basics of modern astrology.

Parkers' Astrology: The Definitive Guide to Using Astrology in Every Aspect of Your Life (2020 edition),
by Julia and Derek Parker
Comprehensive and well-illustrated. The ideal book (after this one!) to deepen your understanding.

The New American Ephemeris for the 21st Century 2000–2100 at Midnight (Michelsen Memorial Edition),
by Neil F. Michelsen and (compiler) Rique Pottenger
Accurate 'timetable' of where the planets are in the zodiac over a 100-year period.

Schools of Astrology

ASTROLOGY UNIVERSITY
astrologyuniversity.com
Excellent tutors and low-cost webinars which you can download.

KEPLER COLLEGE
keplercollege.org
Highly regarded school with courses introducing the fundamentals of astrology.

LONDON SCHOOL OF ASTROLOGY
londonschoolofastrology.co.uk
Offers evening classes and Saturday seminars.

THE MAYO SCHOOL OF ASTROLOGY
mayoastrology.com
Runs correspondence courses with plenty of video conference tuition.

Acknowledgments

Author Biographies

Victor Olliver (author) is a leading UK-based practitioner and teacher of astrology who has edited the Astrological Association's prestigious magazine *The Astrological Journal* since 2014. With a distinction diploma in astrology from London's Mayo School, he is the author of the *Lifesurfing* annual forecast books and *Chasing the Dragons: An Introduction to Draconic Astrology*. Astrologer to *The Lady*, he has lectured in the US, Australia, South Africa and many parts of Europe, and is Media Officer of the Association of Professional Astrologers International which regulates ethical standards in astrology. Website: victorolliver.co.uk.

Shelley von Strunckel (foreword) is an astrologer, writer, speaker and, most recently, celebrity-influencer. Her daily, weekly, monthly and yearly columns are published worldwide, and are also available on her website (www.shelleyvonstrunckel.com). Hollywood-born and based in Kings Cross, London, her background combines business and spiritual studies; she blends both in her astrological columns, speaking and media appearances. Shelley emphasizes the power that comes with exploring astrology's insights, for individuals, in business, in leading a fulfilling life and in healing the planet to create a new, harmonious world, for today and the future.

Picture Credits

Special thanks to all the contributors to this book: © **Tuyet Dinh Sinh Vat** 34; astrological charts and symbols from Solar Fire 9 with permission of **Astrolabe Inc** (https://alabe.com/): 38, 96, 99, 100. Courtesy of **Shutterstock.com** and © the following, in page order: Daryaart9 1 & 2 & 128; Jozef Klopacka 3 & 42, 65, 84; Ola-ola 4; Tithi Luadthong 6; yoshi0511 7; BasPhoto 8; Bada1 9; Sahroe 10; agsandrew 11, 27, 41, 47, 73, 78, 79, 89, 92, 125; sarayut_sy 12; Tokarchuk Andrii 13; Anastasiya Smolina 14, 15, 18, 19, 20, 21, 22, 24, 25, 35; WinWin artlab 14 & 15 & 16 & 16 & 18 & 19 & 20 & 20 & 21 & 22 & 24 & 24; AnastasiaOsipova 16, 18, 21; Nomad_Soul 17; Zvereva Yana 23; Peratek 26; Bruce Rolff 28, 31, 68, 102, 113; Aleksey Ignatenko 29; wacomka 30; canbedone 32; Sonya92 33; Mio Buono 36; sarayut_sy 37; SEABOY888 39; Oksistyle 40; Dotted Yeti 44, 57; Jorm S 45, 51, 52, 69, 71; Nataliia Zhekova 48; luboffke 50; CC7 53; Peter Hermes Furian 54 & 57 & 58 & 58 & 59 & 61 & 61 & 62 & 62 & 90; jdrv_art 55; Susanitah 56; Kiril_Ph 58; Ezgi Erol 59; SN VFX 59, 61, 72, 119; sickmoose 60; NASA images 62; Vadim Sadovski 63; lolloj 64; Mari Dein 66; Marina Grau 67; PLotulitStocker 70; MoVille 74; pixelparticle 75; Victoria Bat 76; Mimma Key 77; Shyntartanya 80; Paolo Gallo 81; Anastasia Mazeina 82; Space creator 83; SUGIHARTO ZHANG 86; andrey_l 87; EkaterinaP 88; Rolling Stones 91; arvitalyaart 93; Warm_Tail 94, 101, 108, 121, 126; paw 97; wpap 98; whiteMocca 100; vchal 103; 42videography 105; Kaspars Grinvalds 106; Tamiris6 109; alexkich 110; Aris-Tect Group 112; sun ok 114; buradaki 115; Joule Sorubou 116; Eisfrei 118; Galkin Grigory 120; EFKS 122; Who is Danny 123.